Chasing Rainbows

DARON KENNETH

authorHOUSE®

AuthorHouse™
1663 Liberty Drive
Bloomington, IN 47403
www.authorhouse.com
Phone: 1 (800) 839-8640

Published by AuthorHouse 09/29/2018

ISBN: 978-1-5462-5673-1 (sc)
ISBN: 978-1-5462-5672-4 (e)

Print information available on the last page.

This book is printed on acid-free paper.

Because of the dynamic nature of the Internet, any web addresses or links contained in
this book may have changed since publication and may no longer be valid. The views
expressed in this work are solely those of the author and do not necessarily reflect the
views of the publisher, and the publisher hereby disclaims any responsibility for them.

Contents

There are a million reasons that I care so much
About Rich. The first and foremost is that he's
My best friend. It doesn't get much simpler or
Easy than that. Then there are the twenty three
Years of Love that come with that much Tyme
Together. I Love him because he's been a part
Of my life for almost half of it. Another reason
That I Love him is because he's so darn handsome.
He has rugged good looks for sure. Another
Reason I Love him so much is because we get
Along so well. We also share the same taste in
Many, many things. We also like to do a lot of
Things together. Another reason is that we both
Enjoy sitting and listening to music together as
Well as watching good movies too. I like to sit
On the couch and hold hands someTymes letting
Him rest his head on my lap. Snuggling is always
A great way to end your day…Everyday.

Antiquing

Antiquing can be a lot of fun. You can find
Antiques in so very many places. You can
Find them at antique malls, yard sale and
Estate sales to name but a few. Rich and
Sue and I Love to go to yard sales and
Estate sale when we get a chance. You
Can find all kinds of special deals if you
Are looking in the right place at the right
Tyme. The only bad thing about antiquing
Is that you have to have the right place to
Put all of your treasures. One of my favorite
Things to find while antiquing are old C.D.s
And records. I am always looking for new
Music to play. Another thing about antiquing
Is that you can go on your free Tyme. You
Don't have to go shopping for antiques on
A regular basis and you can keep your eyes
Open for certain things that you're looking
For. Antiquing is a personal thing because
Everybody has their own taste in things
That they are looking for. My favorite
Antiques are old radios and stereos. I just
Love looking for that special piece to put
In the Living room.

As the Clouds Roll By

I look up to the sky as the clouds roll by
Seeing the sun's just like having an eye in the sky
The sun is shining and the sky is blue
When it's not cloudy the sun shines through
Everyone's happy when the sun shines bright
A sunny day makes everything alright
The puffy clouds look like cotton candy
Seeing shapes in the clouds makes me feel dandy
It's nice now that the grass is green
It's the nicest lawn I've ever seen
Maybe I'll sit on the porch with my cat
I know he'll be happy about that
He just Loves to sit in the sun
It's a great way to have some fun
Or maybe we'll just go for a walk
It's always nice to walk and talk
When we're done we'll find our way back
And when we're through we'll have a snack
In the afternoon we'll mow the grass
A great way to make the afternoon pass.

Outside the streets are wet and cold as I sit
Here alone just wishing you were here next
To me. Cold, gray skies seem to be the way
Things are going as of lately. Winter's still
Reigning over the weather as I wait for
Spring to get here and shower me with warmth
And sunlight. When it gets to be like this
For so long I wonder if the seasons will ever
Change for the better. Today is just one of
Those days that is but never should be. I
Look to the skies and wonder if the sun will
Ever shine through all the gloom again. It's
Been hard to think that it's been months since
We've felt the sun on our faces and felt warm
And happy. We are all in need of some sun-
Shine and warm weather. I long to just sit in
The warm sun and feel some pleasant days
Again. Maybe tomorrow? Tomorrow just
Seems like it is eons away. God knows we
All just wish the days would go from sad and
Gloomy to bright, warm and sunny. We all
Just wish the nice weather would return and
Make us all feel happy go lucky once again
And bring a smile to all of our faces.

Best Friends

She's my best friend in the world
She's the nicest pal and girl,
We talk on the phone each day
We've always got a lot to say,
When I pick up the phone she'll be there
We've always got a lot to share,
She does massage and she does nails
I write stories and tell great tales,
Together we're great, together we're good
We get along like best friends should,
My name is Daron and she is Irene
We're the best of friends you've ever seen.

The blue sky above is the color of my heart
When you are not around. I am in a constant
State of sadness when I can't be with you. I
Never thought I would want someone all of the
Tyme…but you make me feel so alive when you
Are around and so alone when you aren't near
Me. I want to have you in my sights all of the
Tyme I am awake and thinking. I am thinking
How lucky I am to have found the one that my
Heart beats for. Each and every moment when
You are not around, I feel like only half of me
Is alive, the other half is in search of the part of
Me that makes me whole and live. From the
Tips of your toes to the top of your head, each
Part of your being is missed when you are not
Near me. I think about you whenever you are
Close and I even think about you whenever I
Don't have you close to me. So stay close to
Me my Love and help my heart be happy and
Whole…once and for always…with you near
To me.

Call Me Cuddles

Shadow has a new nickname: Cuddles. It seems
So appropriate for the cuddly little buddy that he
Is. He has all the traits of a little black Teddy bear.
He's shiny and fuzzy, black and warm, but most
Of all he has the cuddliest personality of all of my
Cats in the past. He's a snuggly little ball of fur
Who just loves it when you play with him. When
He's not playing, he's hunting for treats and a hug
Or two. His golden eyes say he's sorry whenever
He's doing something that he shouldn't be doing.
He Loves to be petted and cuddled like the kitten
That he still is a heart. He has the softest little
Pads on the bottom of his feet, along with some
Dagger like claws. We get his nails clipped on a
Regular basis. When he isn't looking for treats,
He is usually taking long winded naps in his little
Bed. He's so cute when he sleeps because he has
A habit of snoring quite loudly when he is having
One of his little dreams. His fur is so soft and plush,
He's like a bundle of fur with great big claws and
Big beautiful shiny eyes. He truly has the best
Demeanor of all of the cats that I have owned. I
Am so thankful to the Humane Society for hooking
Me up with such a great little guy.

Christmas is Here

With snowflakes falling everywhere
And Christmas Carols filling the air.
Twinkling lights and pretty sights
Make our hearts feel especially light.
It's about giving and sharing
It shows us that you are caring.
Aunt Mary's fruitcakes are on the way
It's Tyme to make your soul feel light today.
Everywhere you look are colors of red and green
The snowy landscape is the best that you've seen.
And Santa will be coming around
You can hear the sleigh bell's twinkling sound.
There are ornaments hanging from the shelves
With presents delivered by Santa's elves.
It's a Tyme for giving cards to friends
Yes, Christmas Tyme is here again!

Christmas Tyme

Oh, Christmas sounds they fill the air
As we remember it's Tyme to give and share,
We see ornaments on every tree
It's a Tyme that fills our hearts with glee,
Santa soon will be coming around
And he'll be in your part of town,
It's a Tyme for giving presents
As we dine on goose, turkey and pheasant,
While children act especially nice
As they go skating on ponds of ice,
Or as they build a man of snow
Our hearts are light wherever we go,
We dress in coats and warm woolen mittens
And in a scarf that grandma's knitted,
Oh, we sing the lovely Christmas songs
That we all Love to sing along,
Oh, twinkling lights and pretty sights
Fill up the eve of this Holy night,
So send your friends some Christmas cards
They're appreciated by whoever you are,
And leave some goodies for Santa's elves
They'll return the thought with gifts on shelves,
This truly is a night that's blessed
As we remember a child that was in swaddling dressed,
Because this is a wonderful Tyme of year
So toast your friends with a cup of cheer.

Cold Winter Days

It's a cold, cold winter's day
It's much to cold to go out and play,
So we stay ourselves inside
Where it's warm and safe and dry,
So I pick up a nice old book
And I start to take a look,
But my mind cannot be found
So I take a good look around,
I put on some music and start to dance
As I get caught up in a trance,
Just listening to old blue eyes
Makes my mood come down to size,
Just listening to him croon
Brings some warmth to this old room,
It just makes me want to fly
Yes, I'll dance until I die.

Cry

SomeTymes I get so down all I want to do is cry,
I hope somehow this might change before I die.
I get to feeling down and I get to feeling all alone,
When I get this way all I want to do is groan.
Nothing brings me up, not even the meds I take,
I hope tomorrow my moods will change before I wake.
There are days I get to feeling dark and gray,
Nothing fixes me, I hate living life this way.
When I'm feeling down I have no appetite,
I wish my moods would swing from wrong to right.
When I'm feeling low, nothing feels any good,
I wish my moods would be the way they should.
There are days that all I want to do is sleep,
I just feel so down, all Tyme ever does is creep.
There are days that all I want to do is dream,
But inside my head all I can do is scream.
I scream that these days will somehow find an end,
But what I really need is to talk to a good friend.
People shy away from you when you're feeling low,
And I feel like I'm some dynamite ready to blow.
I just can't seem to shake these demons in my head,
SomeTymes they get so loud all I wish is I was dead.
Maybe one day soon I'll be happy one more Tyme,
But until that day my days just slowly drift on by.

When I was young, like a lot of boys my
Age, I was in cub scouts. I had the great
Luck of having my mom be the den mother.
She was very creative and would have us
Do things that were fun for kids. We would
Do skits and make projects for our families
To enjoy. One of the best gifts we made
That took old Christmas cards and varnished
Them onto wood that had been stained and
A fixture added so they could be hung on a
Wall or door frame. We also did many skits
That we would perform at den meetings. I
Always enjoyed playing different parts in
The plays. I always had fun even though
Some of the other scouts weren't very well
Behaved. We would get together one day a
Week after school and have our den meetings.
My friend Andy's mom was the other den
Mother. Between the two mothers we had
A lot of fun. I really liked the cub scout
Uniforms to the meetings. They were my
Two favorite colors blue and gold.

David

David and I were once in Love
A man I thought was from heaven above
David and I were such good friends
I thought it would be that way till the end.

David and I were once so close
And then he left leaving me morose
David and I were close by phone
Then he left me all alone.

We'd have fun just us two
He'd bring me up when I was blue
Then one day things all changed
Both our lives were rearranged.

We'd laugh have fun from dusk till dawn
We'd laugh until the night was gone
We'd have fun just us two
He'd make me laugh till I was blue.

Dear Dad,
I Love you. You meant so very much to me
As I grew up and older. I know things weren't
Always copasetic with us in your last few years,
But I tried. I know you weren't a happy person
For much of the Tyme. I know that you drank
To escape your unhappiness, as did many people
Of that generation. It was a Tyme before people
Were treated for their depression and mental
Illness. I enjoyed our Tymes we went fishing
Together and I enjoyed the Tymes we went out
Hunting for squirrels and rabbits. I'm sorry if I
Disappointed you. I always tried my best to
Impress you, but often I felt short of the mark.
We were very different from one another, as I
Was into band and the theater. That was how I
Tried to make people happy, through my acting
And playing in the band. I'm sorry we weren't
Close those last few years of your life. I tried
Often to talk with you but you wouldn't listen.
I know you were stuck in oblivion those last
Few years that you drank. I wanted you to be
Proud of myself, Dana and mom. We all Loved
You so very much, I just hope you realized that.
I hope now that you are free you can look back
And see how much Love there was for you.
Goodbye, and may you have peace now and
Forever more.

Do What's Right

Peace is often hard to find
When there's so much going on,
So seek out Tymes when there is rest
Don't let life steer you wrong.

Never wander far away
Stay yourself close to home,
There is so much to see close by
So keep your eyes open when you roam.

Learn what you have to know
Don't lead a life of sorrow,
There is so much for you to learn
When you live life for tomorrow.

Life is quite chaotic
There is so much to do,
Take every moment as it comes
And sleep when your life is through.

Don't be afraid of living
Open your eyes, don't be shaken,
There is so much for you to behold
Life is grand when you awaken.

There is so much for you to behold
Always seek the light,
Always do what's necessary
And always do what's right.

SomeTymes life can be quite depressing
Leaving you feeling oh, so low,
You have to fight to stay alive,
But just don't let it show.
There are Tymes when life can be chaotic
It leaves you feeling manic,
You can't keep up the pace
But just don't start to panic.
Often life seems out of your control
Leaving you all alone and sad,
Just try to keep a smile on your face
Don't get all alone and mad.
There are Tymes your feet feel off the ground
Leaving you alone and ready to fly,
Don't let life take over your mind
Give God a chance to try.

Down and Blue

I'm feeling down and I'm feeling blue
I'm so sad I don't know what to do,
I miss the sun and I miss the light
I need the sun to make me feel alright,
I sit alone in a darkened room
All I can do is feel the gloom,
I wish the sky wasn't so gray
How I wish it was a sunny day,
Oh, how I wish that you were here
I just need to feel your heart so near,
What I need from you is a real good kiss
A kiss from you would fill me with bliss,
I'm afraid I'll never feel good again
I'm so glad you're my best friend,
I'm so sad all I can do is cry
I know I'll Love you till the day I die,
I'm feeling down and I'm feeling sad
Perhaps one day soon I'll be feeling glad,
Being sad is never funny
I'll feel better when it gets sunny,
I'll hear you when you're calling
I'll catch you when you're falling,
I just miss having you around
To your heart I'm forever bound.

Falling in Love

Everyone dreams of falling in Love and when
They do they want to be friends with the one
They fall in Love with. I have had the good
Fortune of falling in Love and having it be with
My very best friend. I know that I am truly
Blessed to be able to get to marry the one that
I Love. We have been married for three years
And together for twenty three years. I think
That we have stood the test of Tyme because
We are such good friends. I Love Richard with
All of my heart. These past twenty three years
Because our relationship is going and growing
On real Love. Real Love only comes along so
Rarely that when you find yourself in it you
Have to hold on for all that you can because
Love is the most powerful emotion that there
Is. When you fall in Love you can feel it in
Your being. It is a feeling that tells you you
Have found the one person that you were
Meant to be with. I thank God every day
For sending me the person I Love the most.
Love truly is a splendid thing.

Fitting In

She sits all alone and never leaves her home.
She says that she doesn't fit in with the rest
Of this crazy world that we live in. She says
That she wants to make some new friends,
The kind who will be there until the end. But
When she doesn't leave her home, she'll just
Continue to be there all alone. She says she
Feels scared of the world out there. Her life
Was never easy, of that she knows for sure.
But she needs to take some chances in order
To find friendship and romances in order for
There to be a whole new world of people and
Things to see. If she doesn't leave her abode
She'll find it's the end of the road. This is
Because Love and relationships won't come
Knocking on her door any Tyme soon don't
You know. So maybe this will be the Tyme
She will see a doctor and take some medication
That might open up a whole new world just
For her to be just like all of the crazy people
She so avoids. No you can't force a person to
Take medication if there is no harm to themselves
Or others, but you can guide them down the road
To discovery and recovery.

Flight

The sun is shining way up in the sky
It makes me wish that I could fly.
I'm tired of living on the cold hard ground
I'd rather fly just to get around.
I hear the sounds of the little birds
I hear them making their little words.
I wish I could fly like they all do
I wish I could get where they're going to.
I'd like to fly from tree to tree
I'd like to fly from you to me.
You make me feel like I could somehow fly
You make me wish that I could somehow try.
I'd like to fly way up to the sun
I'd like to fly just to have some fun.
Staring into the sky puts me into a trance
I can't fly so I'll just have to dance.

Girls, Girls, Girls

When I was just a little boy, I was always
Depressed when I had to go to school. The
Kids at school never included me in their
Sports activities. Because of this I ended
Up playing with the girls at recess. I was
Never good at any physical activities like
Baseball or football, so I learned how to
Jump rope and play hopscotch. I did
However have one special friend who
Wasn't good at sports either. His name
Was Tracy. Tracy and I played games that
We invented, most of which were about
Magic or having psychic powers. We
Used to pretend that we were aliens from
Space. Our favorite thing to do was to
Watch old horror movies on Friday nights.
Tracy was my very best friend. I never
Cared that I couldn't fit in with the other
Boys at school because I had Tracy to
Hang out with. We always had all of the
Girls to hang out with too. It's funny to
This day most of my friends are women
And that's just fine with me.

Someone once said you can count your
Real friends on one set of hands. Those
Are the friends that you can count on in
An emergency, or when you really need
Them. If you have more than that consider
Yourself to be very blessed. I can count
My real friends on four fingers. That
Doesn't count my family either. Family
Should be there regardless. I'm glad I
Can say that I have four really old friends.
Old friends are just that, friends that have
Been by your side for ages. They aren't
Fair-weather friends, they are there all the
Tyme. They are there for you whenever
You need them regardless of whether
Your life is good and you're having a
Great day or not. Old friends are the
Ones you can rely on when things get
Tough and you're not doing so well or
Not. They are there to share in the good
Tymes and the bad Tymes. They will
Always be your friend regardless of the
Weather.

Goodbye to You

Today I say goodbye to someone I looked
Up to and respected very much. It was
Cancer that took him before his Tyme.
He was my favorite uncle. I respected him
Because when our extended family got
Together he would celebrate but he never
Got impaired in the way some people always
Did. No, he was a great man. I Love his
Children and hold them in the utmost
Respectful way. We always had a good
Tyme whenever it was that we got together.
They were always so much fun to hang
Around with. I Loved the farm where they
Lived. I was always envious of their property
Out in the country. It had lots of space to
Get lost and play in. One of my favorite
Memories of him was when we got together
And butchered a bunch of chickens. I so
Clearly remember it because after a chicken's
Head is cut off they still run around because
It doesn't know that it is dead. I remember
Running away from the chickens because I
Was wearing white pants that day. Need I
Say more? There was blood all over my
Pants... I was extremely grossed out by it
To this day. Goodbye my dear uncle, may
You find your way to heaven.

Green, So Green

Green, Green, the world is so green
As footprints show where I have been.
Two feet and ten toes in the Summer's sand
The water washes over my body so tanned.
Two legs carry out my body now wading
Then back to a blanket of colors fading.
It's colors disappearing in the Summer's sun
While now the clouds over passing has begun.
As I take a long walk on Silver Lake's pier
To the sound of water's dancing I hear.
Then I take a long dive into the fresh lake water
Chasing after a tossed in quarter.
I retrieve the coin then toss it once again
While I swim around where it once had been.
Then finally I make my way to the shore
And lay in the wonderful sun once more.

Halloween

Halloween is finally here
It's a night of dread and fear,
Candles make pumpkins shine bright
As we fill the eve with fear and fright,
Scary creatures are everywhere
As screams and shouts fill up the air,
Kids go door to door seeking treats
Like candy and good things to eat,
Scary decorations are all over the scene
As black cats look so scary and mean,
We have Halloween parties at our school
When we dress up like witches and ghouls,
Everywhere are vampires and ghosts
With demons and monsters from coast to coast,
Scary movies are on T.V.
As ghost stories fill our hearts with glee,
Spooky costumes give us a scare
As screams and groans fill up the air,
Children pull pranks upon their neighbors
While searching for some treats and favors.

Happy Birthday

Birthdays are a special day
A day to celebrate in many ways
It's my favorite day of the year
A day that's filled with Love and cheer.

A day to share with special friends
A day that's fun from start to end
A day that's fun for girls and boys
A day that's filled with lots of joy.

It's a day that's filled with cake and fun
It's lots of fun for everyone
A day that's fun with lots of treats
A day that's fun and really neat.

A day you get gifts from those you Love
A day that's made by God above
It's the day that you were born
It's a day that's not forlorn.

Many years ago when I was about nine years old,
My sister and I would go places together. She
Liked her Winter boots and refused to quit wearing
Them even though the seasons had changed from
The Tyme of year when you wore them to keep
Warm. So much so that she only took them off
At night to go to sleep. Despite everyone begging
Her to stop wearing them and wear her Summer
Shoes, she wore them everywhere she went. It
Was quite the fashion statement to see her wearing
Shorts and Summer shirts and wearing a pair of
Boots that came almost to her little five year old
Knees. The other thing that she liked to do was
Carry a little sandwich bag of hot dogs with her
Wherever she went in case she got hungry. She
Loved to take one out of the bag and acted like
It was a cigar. She would hold them up to her
Mouth and say, "Hello there my little chickadee!"
Just like W.C. Fields would do in his old black
And white movies. The only redeeming factor
Was that regardless of the season was that she
Was always ready to go walking in the rain and
Go puddle jumping.

I Love you because you're so cute.

I Love you because you're so friendly.

I Love you because you're so passionate.

I Love you because you're so cuddly.

I Love you because you're so kind.

I Love you because you're so fine.

I Love you because you're so wonderful.

I Love you because you're so sweet.

I Love you because you're so smart.

I Love you because you're so thoughtful.

I Love you because you're so honest.

I Love you because you're so sincere.

I Love you because you're so motivated.

I Love you because you're so wise.

I Love you because you're so caring.

I Love you because you're so trustworthy.

I Love you because you're so special.

I Love you because you're so unique.

I Love you because you're so talented.

I Love you because you're so handsome.

I Love you because you're so diligent.

I Love you because you're so strong.

I Love you because you're so amazing.

I Love you because you're so awesome.

I Love you because you're so cool.

I Love you because you're so you.

Ice Skating

One of my fondest memories of Winter is ice
Skating at a park as a teen. We would all
Get bundled up and put on our skates and
Skate over to the pond that would get all
Frozen over in the winter. We would all
Skate around the pond playing crack the
Whip. It was so beautiful with all of the
Snow and ice everywhere. All cold and
Icy and bright. The park had warming
Rooms where you could go and warm up
If you felt cold and frozen. We would go
To someone's house afterwards and we
Would drink hot chocolate to warm up
After an afternoon of frozen bliss. The
Pond is large enough to accommodate a
Large number of skaters. I Loved just
Skating for hours. I could skate forwards
But I could never figure out how to skate
Backwards. I remember trying many Tymes
But I could skate best skating forwards.
I Love to get going really fast and then
Skate into a circle to finish.

If I Could Be a Tree

If I could be a tree,
How happy I would be,
Children jumping in my leaves
My limbs blowing in the breeze.
If I could be a pool
That would be so cool,
Kids swimming in my waves
On real hot summer days.
If I could be a cat
I'd be cool with that,
I'd be catching mice
That would be quite nice.
If I could be a frog
I'd rest upon a log,
Or sit on lily pads
That wouldn't be too bad.
If I were a snake
A hissing sound I'd make,
I'd hunt around for food
That would be real good.
If I were the sun
I'd shine for everyone,
I'd keep everybody hot
Now that would hit the spot.
If I were some wine
I'd make everyone feel fine,
How happy I would be
Come have a drink on me.
If I were a book
I hope inside you'd take a look,
I'd spell right every word
And be the sweetest story you've ever heard.

I'll always Love You

I Love you because you're so kind
I Love you because you give me peace of mind
I Love you because you're so fine
I Love you because you're all mine
I Love you for your gentle touch
I Love you because you smile so much
I Love you because you share in our Love
I Love you because you're as gentle as a dove
I Love you for your gentle kiss
I Love you because you bring me bliss
I Love you for your hugs at night
I Love you because you make me feel alright
I Love you for our bond today
I Love you because our Love won't fade away.

I'll Build a Snowman

I think I'll go out and build a snowman today
I guess it's Tyme to go outside and play
Nothing's going to get in my way
I think I'll go out and build a snowman today.

I'm rolling out great big balls of snow
I'll put them where they need to go
I'll sit back and watch them grow
I'm rolling out great big balls of snow.

I need some coal to make his face
I'll put them on with style and grace
He has a smile but just a trace
I need some coal to make his face.

Now he's all made so we can dance
It's fun just to move around and prance
Dancing with him puts me in a trance
Now he's all made so we can dance.

So now we sit back and watch it snow
I sit back and watch the piles grow
Will it ever stop snowing I don't know
So now we sit back and watch it snow.

In a Cage

A clear blue sky on a blue, blue day
Maybe I'll try to run away
Nothing to do on a day like today.
I'm feeling down here in a hole
Trying to feel better is my goal
Being alone is taking its toll.
Feeling alone is making me sad
I'm feeling alone and feeling so bad
I'm trying to reverse this life I've had.
Today I'm feeling old, I'm feeling my age
Feeling so alone, like I'm locked in a cage
Being all alone leaves me full of rage.
I'm feeling bogged down yet I want to fly
Feeling so down today, so I'll give it a try
I never seem to win, guess I'll have a good cry.
But I can't fly, I guess I'll never win
I'm feeling as low as I've ever been
I'm feeling so alone feels like I'm giving in.
There's not much further that I can bend
I hope my broken mind will mend
And if it won't I've come to my end.
There's not much more than I can take
I'm bending as far as I can break
May God save my soul for goodness sake

In Love with You

I feel you deep within my heart
It's been that way right from the start
I long to see your Loving smile
It's been that way for quite a while.

There are Tymes I long to hold your hand
I'm so glad that you're my man
You're so gentle as a dove
You're the one I'll always Love.

You're the one I long to kiss
When you're not here it's you I miss
I'm in heaven when you're holding me
Holding you sets my soul free.

I am so in Love with you
You bring me up when I am blue
I Love the things we do together
Loving you makes me feel better.

You bring me up when I am sad
You make me happy, you make me glad
You truly are my guiding light
Being with you makes me feel right.

Irene

Irene is my best friend. She's been my best
Friend for forty years now. We became best
Friends back in eighth grade. She's the one
I turn to when I need to hear the truth. When
I'm down I know I can count on her to bring
Me out of my depression. And when I'm manic
I can count on her to bring me down to Earth.
We can spend hours talking about nearly nothing
Of importance just because we enjoy each other's
Company. And even when Tyme had come in
Between us we knew that we'd pick up right
Where we left off the last Tyme that we spoke.
I am so proud to have her in my life.

He sleeps alone in his kitty bed, oblivious
To the world going on all around him...
SomeTymes as he has his little cat dreams
His fur is ebony with a few white hairs and
His fur is smooth and shiny as he bathes
Himself. He is a solid sturdy cat, no doubt
About that. He is stark and strong. He has
Big ears that catch every sound around him.
His claws are sharp as daggers to catch and
Claw at his prey as he searches the premises
For vermin. He Loves going out on the porch
And just laying in a big chair absorbing the
Sun as it shines all around him.

It's Spring Tyme

The sun is out, the sky is bright
It's Tyme to stop and enjoy the light,
The grass is brown but it will soon be green
It will be the nicest lawn you've seen,
The trees stand alone, their branches are bare
But they'll soon be covered with leaves everywhere,
The park is empty, it stands alone
It will soon be filled with children that roam,
School is in, but it will soon let out
The streets will be filled with kids all about,
The beaches are closed but they'll be filled to the brim
They'll be overflowing with kids that swim,
The campground is empty, the ground is damp
It will soon be filled with people that camp,
The nearby pond is empty, there's no one to fish
So skip a stone and cast your wish,
Because Winter is over, there's nothing to fear
It's Spring the nicest Tyme of the year.

Jeanie

My friend Jeanie is always by my side.
She is always there if I need to talk.
She has been my friend for twenty nine
Years. Not many of my friends can
Say that, but she can. She's always
There if I need to talk about anything
And everything. She's the kind of
Friend I can count on when the going
Gets good or bad and rough. I know
That if I need her she's just a phone
Call away. Just seven digits and I
Know she's there. She's been there
With me through three relationships.
She's been there through my father's
Volatile years when he was alive and
Right there after in his passing. She
Has been there through many rounds
Of upset with my sister and continues
To be there whether Dana and I are
Getting along or not. She's been there
When my mom started working in
Madison and I expect her to be there
Through her retirement as a house
Mother too. She's someone I can
Always count on to be there and I
Hope she'll be there till my days
Are over.

I looked up to see the sun, but it was just another
Cloudy day as usual for this Tyme of year. I took
A look around the streets and noticed it was a nice
Neighborhood. The houses are well kept. The street
Doesn't get a lot of traffic ever. I hope it stays the
Nice neighborhood that it is right now. I decided to
Go and get the mail. Just some bills and more junk
Mail. I walked to the back porch and sat on one of
The loungers. This made me remember all the good
Tymes that these old loungers had seen. They are
Still comfortable after all these years. I saw some
Birds flying into the hedge next door. I thought it
Must be nice to be able to fly wherever you want
To go. I heard an airplane overhead. I remember
That that happens a lot around here being so close
To the airport. I thought to myself, if I could fly
I'd fly to wherever it is nice all Tymes of the year
Not just this Tyme of the year. I thought to myself
That will never happen, so I'll just take a little nap
On my favorite furniture. And that's just what I did.

I look up to the sky to see my dad
Missing him just makes me feel so bad
I stare up into the sky so bright
SomeTymes I get blinded by the light
I look up to see him in the clouds
I miss him when I think aloud
I think I see him in the skies
Or whenever I see butterflies
I miss him when I'm feeling alone
I wish I could call him on the phone
There are Tymes I wish that we could talk
Or that we could just go for a walk
I wonder what he sees when he looks down
I hope he's not looking at me with a frown
I Look up and I see a dove
A symbol of undying Love
I know God holds him in his hand
Knowing he's with God makes me feel grand.

Every day is a new day to tell you just how
Much I Love you....And a new chance to
Show you just how much you mean to me.
I try to let you know that you are my whole
World and more. You are the single most
Important part of my world and I Love you
For it. You mean so much to me, so much
More than I ever thought I could Love and
Care for someone again. After my last
Relationship broke up, I swore that I would
Never let someone back into my life, and I
Would never allow myself to care for anyone
Else again, but with you it was easy. You
Came into my world and made each and every
Day better than the last. With each day that
Passes I grow to Love you more than the last.
Thank you for teaching me that Love wasn't
A part of my life that I had given away and
Forgotten. You are the reason that I wake in
In the morning, and you are the reason I have
To go to sleep each night and dream about us.
You have given me a reason to carry on each
Day, something I thought would never happen
Again. Thank you for being the light in my
Life that keeps me alive. You are the reason
I live for, breathe for, and dream of...YOU.
You make me live a life I had only dreamed
Of . Thank you for making my life complete.

Whenever you are near I fall in Love all over
Again. You are so very thoughtful in all that
You do for me as well as others. You do all
The wonderful things that make it so easy to
Love you in so many, many ways. I want to
Have you in my life so that I can feel completed.
A life without you in it would be nothing but
Boring and bland. You put your kind heart in
To all that you do, making life so much more
Special and splendid. When you're not around
My life seems so useless. I Love spending my
Free Tyme with you because you make my life
Meaningful and so much more exciting. You're
Handsome good looks make it so easy to Love
You all the more. I Love spending Tyme with
You and doing things with you because you
Make life fun. You're the kind of person who
Can take something plain and simple and make
It uniquely yours and special. I Love you for
All that you are and all that you do. Thank you
For making my life all the more beautiful by just
Being in it. Thank you for just being yourself.

Just Me and Just You

It's nice and sunny outside today
I think I'll go outside and play
Something to do on a nice warm day.
The clouds are out and the sky is blue
There are so many things that you can do
We'll have some fun just me and you
There are so many ways to have some fun
SomeTymes it's just nice to sit in the sun
If I'm really ambitious I might go for a run.
I just might go out and work on the lawn
When the weather's so nice from dusk till dawn
I'm so glad the Winter's finally gone.
When I get done It's you that I'll hold
Just Loving you makes me feel bold
Just Loving you is better than gold.
And when the day's gone I'll turn on the light
You're smiling face makes everything bright
I'll give you my Love with all of my might.

Kitten Life

Shadow sleeps all snuggled up in his bed.
As he sleeps he purrs a little every so often.
When he wakes he yawns and stretches a
Little bit. He looks all around to find what
To do to make his next move. Slowly he
Creeps out of his bed and decides to go over
To his water dish and have a quick drink
Followed by munching on some of his food.
After he finishes he comes over to me and
He rubs against my legs telling me that he
Loves me. I pick him up and set him on my
Lap, but he doesn't stay there for long. He
Is definitely not a lap cat like Buzzers and
K.D. were. He is still just a kitten so he
Would rather play than just sit around on my
Lap. I throw his ball for him to chase around.
For some reason I always forget that he isn't
A dog and he won't fetch like a puppy will.
After I've thrown the ball a few Tymes he
Comes to me and lets me pet him by rubbing
His ears and scratching his face a little. Then
I do the one thing that he can't resist and shake
His treats bag and he goes crazy for the little
Bits of kibble that I give him. Then when he
Gets done eating he goes quietly back to his
Bed for another nap or two. Boy, being a
Kitten sure is a lot of work!

My mother has never remarried since she and
My father divorced many years ago. She has
Someone very special in her life. His name is
Marlo. Marlo would be my stepfather if she
Ever got married again. She and Marlo have
Been together some thirty plus years. They
Go everywhere and do everything together. I
Know that Marlo makes her very happy. He
Treats my mother like a queen. I must say
That I am so happy that she has found her very
Special soul in Marlo. I don't know anyone
That tries to make her happier than Marlo does.
I hope that they will get married and walk
Down the aisle together. But if that doesn't
Happen I know that they are very happy and
Content just the way they are now. Marlo
Is a perfect match for my mom because he
Is a very giving and kind soul just like she is.
That's two very giving and kind people. You
Can't go wrong with a match up like that.
Mom and Marlo go everywhere and do every
Thing together. They Love to just spend the
Day driving around the country side. They
Also enjoy fishing a lot together. I am so very
Happy to see them with one another. I would
Be very proud to call Marlo my dad.

We sit on the couch together every day. (just
Sitting with him makes me feel better). He
Likes to get his ears and belly rubbed, and
When he's happy he just purrs and purrs.
He gives himself a bath several Tymes a day.
Shadow Loves to eat, especially cat treats.
We Love to watch T.V. together, especially
Shadow. He stares at the T.V. screen. He
Loves to sneak out the door, but I can always
Get him back by shaking the treats jar. Sneaky
Me, I always get him back every Tyme. He
Really enjoys sleeping in his cat bed, but even
More when he sleeps with Richard and I.
Shadow hasn't learned to "meow" yet. I hope
He'll figure it out someTyme soon so we can
Communicate in that way. Shadow likes giving
Me little cat kisses and I return the favor by
Kissing him on his nose. He Loves to eat all
Of the Tyme…his food and my house plants
As well. He adores racing through the house
At full speed, (I swear he's going to fly through
The wall and out the door.) He likes playing on
The porch and patio as well. His favorite thing
To do is have me hold him on his back and nuzzle
Nose to nose like a baby. He is just a growing
Kitten and I Love him to death.

A wise man once said that when thoughts
About those who are no longer with us
Come to the forefront of our thoughts, it
Is because we need to say a prayer for
Those persons. I couldn't agree more.
I have thought about all the wonderful
People who were for whatever reason
Taken from us too early that we need
To remember them be cause they aren't
Here to share with us anymore. They
Are lost but not forgotten. We need
To remember all of the wonderful things
That they shared with us while they were
Here. Some of the most beautiful souls
That I know were taken from us due to
The AIDS crisis of the 80's and 90's.
But for that reason they might still be
Here making the world a better place.
I lost too many friends due to the HIV
Epidemic. I think of all the good Tymes
That we had together. It is sad that so
Many special people were taken way
Too soon. I think of them and the many
Friendships that were lost because of
The horrible disease that is AIDS. I
Know that wherever they are, they are
Looking down and reminding us to
Remember their Love, friendship and
Wonderful things that they brought with
Them to this life. Even if it was just for
A short Tyme.

Sitting all alone in a darkened room, just sitting
Here I'm feeling full of sadness. Just missing
You is all I can do. I'm wishing you were here
Next to me today so I could hold you and feel
Your Love. Seems like it's been forever since
We've been together. Your Love seems Like
It's miles away. I need to hold you and know
You're still here for me. SomeTymes all I need
Is to hold your hand in mine. When I do, every-
Thing starts to make sense again. When you're
Not here the world seems to make no sense at
All. You're the piece of the puzzle that makes
Everything come together. When I get to hold
You all my troubles and worries seem to disappear
Even if just for a little while. When I get to kiss
You I know that I can make it through even the
Most troubling of days, even if it's just one day
At a Tyme. So please hold me in your arms so
I can make it through another sad day like this
One.

Music

Music is my way of life
Music tears me from my strife
Music makes of breaks a mood
Music leaves you feeling good.

Music comes in many styles
Music makes me an audiophile
I Love music night and day
I Love music in so many ways.

Music is always pleasant to hear
Music helps you cope with fear
Music leaves you feeling proud
Music is best when it's heard loud.

Music can be just one voice
Music types come in many a choice
Music helps when you are feeling mad
Music cheers you up when you are sad.

My Guiding Light

Holding you makes me feel so good
When you hold me in the way you should
You're truly my guiding light
Being with you makes me feel right.

I Love it when you're by my side
I'll let you be my Loving guide
By you're side's where I long to be
Being in Love sets my heart free.

Even when I'm down and feeling blue
You always know exactly what to do
I just want to hold you near
You're the one I Love so dear.

To your heart I'm forever bound
I just Love having you around
I hope to seen you soon again
Because you are my Loving friend.

With your heart I'm sure to fly
I'll be with you till the day I die
Our Love begins with just one kiss
Your heart fills my heart with bliss.

My Light

You're my wonderful Loving guide
I long to have you by my side.
You're so handsome you're so true
You bring me up when I'm feeling blue.

You're the one I want to have beside me
You're also the one I long to guide me
When I'm sad I long to hold your hand
Holding you makes me feel so grand.

Making Love to you takes my breath away
I want to be at your side both night and day
Want to hold you when I'm feeling sad
Just Loving you makes me feel glad.

You're the one I hold deep in my heart
I know that I've Loved you from the start
If I'm a tree then you're my roots
I Love you because you're so darn cute.

I long for you when I'm all alone
If you're in my heart then you're my home
When it's late at night you are my light
You always make me feel so right.

My Mom

My mother is a very special lady. She works
As a sorority mom in Madison, Wisconsin.
She works very hard each and every day to
Make sure the girls have a great day each
And every day. She is my very best friend
As well. She is a very kind and Loving soul
As well. She is one of the best souls I have
Ever known. She is a very giving person
And is always easy to get along with. I am
Very lucky to have such a beautiful soul in
My life. Because she is always there for
Everybody in her life she is someTymes
Taken advantage of by those who seek her
Kindness and goodness of heart. She is the
Kind of person who never stops to worry
About what others think because she has
So many people to take care of in her life.
She is the kind of person who will stop and
Buy a homeless person something to eat if
They are hungry. She treats everybody in
Her life with great respect. She is truly the
Most kind and Loveable person I have ever
Known. I am so proud to call her my mother
And friend. Her name is Shirley.

My Purring Friend

He lays there in his kitten's bed
As I speak the words that I have said,
I seek to make him close to me
So I call out his name Tymes three.
He perks up his little ears
He is so cute, he is so dear,
As he begins to wash himself
I pick his treats up off the shelf.
He hears the sound as I shake the bag
He comes so close, he doesn't lag,
He is so cute my furry friend
As kisses to him I softly lend.
He's such a card, he is so funny
As he sits there in the window sunny,
He rubs his back, he begins to purr
A cat is so much cooler than a cur.
After he eats and his treats are gone
He lays back down and begins to yawn,
He now begins to go back to sleep
Just napping the day as minutes creep.

No More Snow!

The sun is out and shining today
It's calling me to come out and play,
There are lots of clouds and the sky is blue
So that's exactly what I'll do,
I'll go out and take a walk
While I'm out I'll stop and talk,
To the people that I see out there
Because the weather's so nice and fair,
I'll take a walk down to the park
I'll be back before it gets dark,
I'm walking because the weather is nice
It's early Spring but no more ice,
I'm happy because there's no more snow
I'm so glad it had to finally go,
It melted and went far from here
So now everyone's full of cheer,
There's so much to do until it gets night
So come on out and enjoy the light.

Oh, Mania!

Oh, mania, you've taken over my life again.
What can I do but ride you out. There is
Nothing on Earth that will slow you down,
Down to a killer speed. Down to the killer
Speed that so many would die for. But oh
Those whose who have been in your presence
Know how relentless you can be to me.
Please take a moment and let me adjust to
That racing pace that you keep. My heart
Races so fast that it is often hard to catch
My breath, let alone my heart beat of a
Million miles a second. My body longs for
That relaxation speed of being down and
Out that depression knows so well. But it
Has its own problems too. SomeTymes the
Rate of being down and out is so slow that
It gets run over by a snail. And just where
Does all that energy come from anyway? I
Feel like I've drank two or three dozen cups
Of coffee and then just being sat down to try
To chill out. I wish I could just let all of this
Energy fly right out of my hands. Just like a
Witch's wand would do. But that's not going
To happen either. Mania, oh mania you wicked
Nasty ride you! Go find someone else to torture
With that wild and racing speed of yours. I
Beg of you, go and haunt someone new. Make
It someone who enjoys life at light speed, but
Not I, not I, not I.

On Some Days

Shadow is my cute little bear
A big black cat with short black hair
I Love your pretty golden eyes
For a cat you are quite wise
You like to stay in your bed all day
And when you're not you like to play
Some days you like to sit in the sun
Getting lots of attention from everyone
Some days you like to chase your tail
Other days you chew up our mail
You're a cat with a great big heart
I know that we will never part
Know my Love for you is true
When you're not here I'm feeling blue
You like eating spiders and ants
And grazing on all my house plants
You're so wise you're a smart boy
Hiding in a bag is you're favorite toy.

Opportunities

There's a lot of opportunities
So live life for every minute,
Don't waste your Tyme in silent repose
Every chance is a way to win it.

The sun rises in the morning
And settles in the night,
So keep your eyes wide open
To win what you just might.

The sun rises in the morning
At night we see the moon,
Life is ever so, so short
Take rest at the Tyme of noon.

Life can be quite crazy
The afterlife comes too soon,
Don't waste a single moment
Rise to the sun sleep by the moon.

Life is very short
Don't be afraid to live,
Share what you have learned
Don't be afraid to give.

The Tyme in your life is fleeting
Your whole life is at stake,
Do what you must to be happy
Just bend but never break.

I'm sitting on my front porch waiting for Spring
To arrive. Last week it was sixty degrees and it
Felt like Spring was here. Not today though, it's
Another day of gray clouds and cold weather. It
Seems like everyone is waiting for Spring to get
Here. The people, the birds, the raccoons and the
Squirrels are waiting for Miss Spring to finally shed
Her Winter clothes and don her Spring Greens for
All to enjoy. I'm so tired of sweat shirts and my
Sweaters warm pants and slippers. It is Tyme for
Us to move on into the months where it is warm
And wonderful with soft clouds and gentle rains
That will bring forth the flowers of Spring and the
Green, green grass on the ground and leaves in the
Trees. The poor cold, naked trees seem to be saying
"Give us something to put on already!" the shovel
For snow is ready to be retired and in its place we
Shall see the lawnmower and gardening tools and
Oh, yes the lawn sprinkler. How could anyone
Forget the joy that a lawn sprinkler brings to the
Children and the lawn itself? I'm so looking forward
To going for little treks around the neighborhood
When the weather is nice and presentable. Mr. Sun
I beg you, come on out and play…We're ready and
Willing and anxious for your return!

Rainbows

If there is no Heaven
Then there is no hell as well,
So live life for the moment
To try to make things swell.

Try to forget about money
Live life for the now
There's nothing but this moment
Let happiness show you how.

Do not live life stagnant
Live for all you know
There's Tyme to sleep in the afterlife
So pay attention as you go.

Keep looking for the rainbows
At the end there's a pot of gold,
Keep searching for your whole life
You'll find it before you're old.

Keep your eyes open at all Tymes
Never let them close,
There's so much to take in in this life
You can shut them when you repose.

Rich

My husband Rich is my closest friend and ally . I
Love him so very, very much. He is always doing
Kind things for others as well as myself. He is
Truly the kindest and best friend I have ever known
In my life. It is easy to see why we get along so well
Because we are both such giving and caring people.
I really Love him for all of the wonderful things he
Does for myself, his family and the others in his
Life. Rich is a very hard worker. He does every-
Thing he can to make Walmart where he works a
Good place to work and shop. Some people get
Mad at him because he holds such high standards
At work. I think it is wonderful that some one takes
His work so seriously. A lot of people don't care
About their jobs but he does. That's rare and hard
To find these days. I am so proud of him. He is a
Very diligent person. He puts his best efforts into
The things that he does. I know that he is the kind
Of person that would be there to help you if you
Needed something. That is also very rare and hard
To find in people today. I am so very proud to call
Him my friend and my husband.

Rocks

When I was a child I used to really enjoy
Going on a hunt for rocks for my rock
Collection. The rocks I liked the most
Were rocks that had shiny crystals in them
I would save them in an old coffee can or
SomeTymes just a bag to put them in. I
Would keep them in a special place. My
Rock collection was one of my favorites
Because there are so many colors, shapes
And sizes of rocks that can be found just
By looking around you. It's funny but I
Would always give the pretty stones to
My mother to keep and she would keep
Them for a couple of days and then I
Would just forget about them and find
Some new rocks to replace the old ones.
I could never figure out where all my
Great rocks were going, but as I got older
I realized mom was just taking all of the
Rocks and just throwing them away. The
Other thing I would do was to varnish
And cover the stones with it. This made
The colors and characteristics of the rocks
Really show up. I would always give the
Prettiest stones away. I never realized that
They weren't worth anything, but saved
Them in my collection just the same.

She picked up the box that was wrapped in birthday
Paper and shook it back and forth. She began to
Unwrap the gift. When she had gotten all of the
Paper off she could see what was in the box it was
Roller skates. She opened the box and pulled the
Skates out and immediately began to try them on.
The fit perfectly. Her mother helped her walk to
The door. She opened the door and began to skate.
She realized that she needed to have good balance
In order to skate properly. She got on the sidewalk
And began to skate on the open cement in front of
Her. She was free! This is easy she thought… and
Fun too. She cruised along the sidewalk and was
Having the Tyme of her life until she hit a crack in
The pavement and fell down at full speed. She got
Up with bloody knees and a bloody elbow. She took
Off the skates and went into the house and placed
The skates back in the box which is right where they
Stayed till the end of her childhood. That was the
End of her skating career.

Sad and Blue

I'm feeling sad and blue today
I'm wishing I didn't feel this way
The weather outside is really bad
Bad weather seems to make me sad
When the weather's bad it makes me blue
I wish there was something I could do
I wish that I could just see the sun
The sun is Loved by everyone
When the weather's bad it makes me cry
Oh how I wish my eyes would dry
Bad weather seems to bring me down
The only thing on my face is a frown
But someday soon the sun will shine so bright
And I'll see the sun and the clouds so white
Then we can go for a walk together
Something fun to do when you have nice weather

Shades of Blue

Everywhere I look, I'm looking for you,
But everything I see are only shades of blue.
And I'm looking for you in the stars,
The ones that shine on full true,
But all that I can see are lonely shades of blue.
I wander the streets,
Alone and without you,
But all that I can see
Are lonely shades of blue.
Shine on blue, shine on blue,
Shine on blue, shine on blue,
I'm shining bright blue for you.
And now as the end comes true,
I'm shining bright blue for you.
Burning blue, burning blue,
I'm burning bright blue for you.
I'm caught up in this haze
And there's nothing else I can do,
I'm burning bright blue, I'm burning bright blue,
I'm a fire that burns bright blue for you.

Curled up I see my Shadow as he sleeps in
A ball on the couch. Slowly his body breathes
In and slowly his body breathes out. Every
Once in a while he opens his eyes to make
Sure all is in its place. Then he drifts off into
His cat dreams. I wonder what he's thinking
As he sleeps on and on into the afternoon. I
Wonder does he dream of catching mice or
Maybe some birds…just what goes on in that
Little head of his. I have noticed that he is
Eating less yet getting bigger in the middle,
Maybe too many treats? I always know when
It is Tyme to take him to the vet to get his
Nails clipped, as he starts clawing at all the
Furniture again and again. Every once in a
While some cars will make some noises as
They drive on by, he perks his ears up and if
It's loud enough he'll get up and move ever
So slightly and then settle back down into his
Dreamland on the sofa. Every once in a while
He will rise up and arch his back just a little,
Then yawn as if the world was all too boring
For him. Then he closes his golden eyes and
Goes back to sleep. Aaaah, what a rough life
He has.

He sits up on the top of the chair
He likes it because he can see from there.
He sits and watches the world go by
He sits and wishes that he could fly.
He has gold eyes and his fur is black
He looks as if he'll make an attack.
He's making a move to come over to me
He's moving to where he wants to be.
He likes to look for the birds outside
He's ready to run and go for a ride.
He sits and behaves so he'll be given some treats
He likes them more than anything that he eats.
He is my most precious boy
He is my most precious toy.
He likes to sit in the windows
He's always happy wherever he goes.
He's always happy wherever he's at
He's always happy that he's my cat.

Shadow walked casually down the steps and
He began to walk out onto the back porch…
As he walked he took in the new environment.
He stalked back and forth along the wall of
Screens and stopped and began to listen to
The sounds of the birds in the hedge. He
Stood up on his back two legs and began to
Look closely at the hedge. He could see all
The birds coming and going and he stared at
It. He got up to the windowsill and paced
Back and forth. The birds were so close that
He could smell them. He tired of just staring
So he walked up to the rug and laid down.
His tail waved to and fro as he looked out the
Other end of the porch. He sniffed along the
Wall of screens, then walked behind the blue
Staircase. He liked it because it was dark back
There and he could hide there, blending into
The darkness. After a while he tired of this
Too and began to squeeze through the opening
At the top of the cellar. He walked up to the
Top of the stairs and laid down for a while, his
Eyes scouring the entire length of the porch.
He walked down the stairs and went back to
His spot on the screen window, just taking in
All of the sights…So many birds, so little Tyme.

Shadow

Shadow lays on a big warm blanket and he
Looks into my eyes. I could see my reflection
In them. He stops and licks his fur and then he
Cleans his paws. His slow gentle breathing
Makes his chest to slowly rise up. Every once
In a while I see his whiskers move as he opens
His mouth and yawns, for it is a lonely afternoon
And it is many hours until his dinner Tyme. He
Slowly swishes his tail back and forth. Every
So often he opens his eyes and I can see those
Gold eyes of his…just wondering what he is
Thinking as he rests his day away like that.
Once in a while a car drives by on the street
And the sounds wake him from his slumber.
He wiggles his nose and then turns away now
Facing the opposite direction. As he sleeps
His ears twitch in different ways to the sounds
He hears out of doors and around the room.
His breathing slows way down and then suddenly
His ears perk up and he checks everything around
Him, and then slowly, ever so slowly he eases
Back to the joys of sleeping once again. He
Returns to his nap and with one last yawn he
Falls into a deep, deep sleep.

When I think of you I fall in Love all over
Again. You are the reason that I live for.
I Love you because you are such a wonderful
Person. You are so giving and so thoughtful
In all that you do. You are always doing nice
Things for me as well. I appreciate you so
Much I couldn't even begin to imagine a life
Without you in it. You take all the ordinary
And make it extraordinary in everything that
You do. You're handsome too. I know that
Your good looks are also a reason that I am
In Love with you. You are kind to everyone
Which is another reason I Love you so much.
Your good demeanor is another thing that I
So enjoy about you. You're the kind of person
I like to spend my Tyme with each and every
Day. You are the kind of person who helps
Make life worth living.

Once many years ago when I was just a little
Tyke, my friends and I were playing hide and
Seek. For some strange reason, I had decided
To hide in the clothes hamper in our bathroom.
I guess it was because I was still young enough
And small enough to fit in there. As it was,
Someone was looking for me and I had made
Some noise and they had found out where I was
So they decided to play a nasty trick on me by
Sitting on top of the hamper. I couldn't get out
Because they were sitting there and keeping me
Stuck in there with no way to get out. I began
To panic and started screaming and yelling for
Them to get off of it and let me out of there. It
Was very dark and cramped in there. I began to
Yell for help but no one could hear me. So I
Started pushing on the top of the hamper, but
They wouldn't budge. Finally after what had
Seemed to be an eternity, they got off of the
Hamper and let me out of there. To this day I
Am still bothered by it when I have to go into
Small and dark cramped spaces. I avoid all
Cramped and little dark spaces and I have panic
Attacks when I have to use elevators as well.
Shame on them for playing a nasty trick on me,
It scarred me for life.

Some Days

Shadow you're my little bear
A big black cat with short black hair,
I Love your pretty golden eyes
For a cat I know you're wise,
You like to stay in your bed all day
And when you're not you like to play,
Some days you like to sit in the sun
Getting attention from everyone,
Some days you like to chase your tail
When you're not chewing up our mail,
I know my Love for you is true
When you're not here I'm feeling blue
I know we'll never be apart
You're a great big cat with a great big heart.

Spring Days

Blue skies say Spring is on the way
Still cold winds make my heart go astray.
The warm sun says it will be Spring soon
It will lift your spirits just like a balloon.
Up in the air the sun is bright and yellow
It will leave you feeling relaxed and mellow.
When Miss Spring comes she'll arrive so fast
That we will know Winter is gone at last.
Soon it will be Tyme to go for a walking
Or just hanging out and doing some talking.
The leaves and the grass will be coming up green
And the flowers will be the prettiest you've seen.
Then baseball comes back into its season
Just watching a game can be so pleasing.
While at the game the grills will be cooking
And at the night stars your eyes will be looking.
Yes, everyone Loves to go outside and play
A great thing to do on a warm Spring day.

Spring Tyme

Spring is starting to come through
The sun is shining through the trees
Spring makes life seem so renewed
I can feel the sunlight in the breeze.

The sun is showing her attention
The grass and leaves are starting to grow
But everywhere you turn and look
The signs of Spring are starting to show.

You can feel the warmth of the sun
Wherever you look the sun is shining through
You can see the clouds up in the sky today
The skies are shining the bright color blue.

So make sure you go for a walk today
Spring Tyme is showing through everywhere
When you do you'll probably see your friends
Get out and smell the Spring Tyme air.

Spring?

I'm feeling sad and down again today. It seems
Like it's been forever since I felt happy and cheerful.
Depression is the norm as of lately. So sad, but very
True. They say April showers can bring May flowers
But it's an awfully long month of rain and discontent-
Ment. Today is just one of those days where you just
Want to curl up with a long nap until the days go by.
But the sun is nowhere to be found today. So I'll
Just snuggle up with my cat while I wait for the nice
Sunny days to get here. If the weather was better it
Would make everyone feel a little more lighthearted.
Why does it take so long for Spring to get here. They
Say Tyme heals all wounds and sadness. I guess we'll
Never know for sure. Until Spring gets here we'll just
Have to muddle through these sad gray and gloomy
Days one by one. Sun? Are you listening? We're just
Waiting for you to come back and lighten our moods
And make us feel Loved when we're bathed in your light.

Sue

My friend Sue is back in my life. There have
Been Tymes when we had gone our separate
Ways because we are both the same type of
Person. The kind who does things for others
And the kind of person who puts others first.
She is a very kind and beautiful soul. I have
Often said that she is my soul sister. But the
Truth of it is that if I wasn't married to Rich
And I was straight, she would be the one that
I would marry. She is one of the few people
In the world today that puts others ahead of
Herself. This is a rare trait in deed. She and
I spend lots of Tyme together enjoying music
Books and movies. We have been friends for
More than twenty years. This is a very special
Relationship not only because we have been
Friends for so long, but also because she means
So very, very much to me. I don't have a lot
Of friends, but the ones that I do have are very
Very important to me. Sue will be retiring soon.
I hope that this will mean we will have more
Tyme together. I Love Sue very much and I am
Looking forward to her new status in life and
Sharing as much of her life with her as I can.

The Kitten in the Drawer

Back many, many years ago…we had adopted
A kitten in our family. The kitten was a cute little
Calico type. We had gotten him from a friend of
The family. He was very rambunctious type of
Kitten. He had gotten into trouble from Tyme to
Tyme. The Tyme that I remember the most was
A Tyme when he had come up missing. We had
Looked all over the house and yard for him. We
Searched high and low for him just wondering
Where he had gotten away to. As it happened
We had sort of given up hope of ever finding him
After he hadn't turned up for three or maybe four
Days and without a clue as to where he might be.
So we were in my sister's room and for some
Strange reason we had stopped talking and she
Had went to her dresser for a pair of socks. We
Opened the drawer to the dresser when we were
Quite pleasantly surprised to see a little bundle
Of fur in the drawer who had just woken up and
Was yawning as if to say, "thanks for the nap and
Finally getting me out of here,". It was our little
Kitten who had been missing and was sitting very
Quietly among the piles of socks in there and was
Ready for something to eat. We were all very
Pleasantly surprised to find him alive and well.
My sister must have put him in there and forgot
Where she had placed him.

The Life I've Had

As I think about the life I've had
I don't know why it makes me feel so sad
I can't stand to feel so bad
I feel so low it makes me mad.

I can't stand to live with this brain
It drives me nuts to be insane
I can't stand to feel this pain
I think I'll lay in front of a train.

I just wish the sun was out
It just makes me want to shout
I can't stand all this chaos about
I hate it because I want to pout.

Sitting on the sun porch as I watch the world go by
I'm sitting on the sun porch and I wish I could fly
Sitting on the sun porch as I give it another try
Sitting on the sun porch I guess I'm not that smart of a guy.

The One

You're the one I Love so much
You're the one I Love to touch,
You're so handsome, you're so strong
Next to you is where I belong.
You're an angel sent from above
You're the one that I'll always Love.
When I'm down, you're the one I miss
Spending Tyme with you fills me with bliss.
I long for you when I'm alone
You're the nicest guy I know.
I want to hold you in my arms
I Love you and your stately charms.
SomeTymes I need to hold your hand
Your gentle touch make me feel grand.
I want to hold you when I cry
I'll Love you till the day I die.
I Love the things that you do for me
Loving you sets my heart free.
I Love having you around
To your heart I'm forever bound.
I Love you because you're so clever
I'll Love you for now until forever.

The Pond in the Middle of the Park

There's a pond in the middle of the park
People go to fish there until it gets dark
In the Winter people go there to skate
They have lots of fun till it gets late
In the Summer kids go there to play
They have fun there each and every day
The kids enjoy swinging on the swings
They swing around like they have wings
There's a baseball diamond where you can play ball
It's a lot of fun in the Spring, Summer and Fall.
There's a seesaw on which you can ride
There's lots of places for you to hide
There's lots of trails for you to walk on
A great place for you to walk and talk on
There's ducks in the pond that you can feed
Just bring some old bread if you feel the need
If you get bored you can sit on a log
If you feel so inclined you can walk your dog
There's a fountain where you can get a drink
And a lot of places to stop and think
It's a very nice place to climb a tree
The best part of the park is it's always free.

The Yoyo Plan

It seems I'm on the yoyo plan again. I don't
Sleep for a few days and then I sleep all around
The clock for a few days to make up for the
Days that I have missed. When you don't sleep
For a few days you get all wierded out and when
You sleep all day for several days you miss out on
What's going on around you. When I'm really
Tired I can try to catch up with some caffeine by
Drinking some tea, but it isn't the same as getting
Some sleep. You're really just flying through
Life on auto pilot and not manning the reins like
You need to be. You really need some good solid
Sleep because if you don't you're not really in
Observance you're just coasting on caffeine, and
Kind of like a robot. I know that a lot of what I'm
Doing isn't being recorded so I can recall it later.
It's important to get the sleep that you need so that
You're on task and remembering the things you need
To get done. The best part of the yoyo plan that I
Get on is that it only lasts for a few days. There
Is nothing worse than going on the yoyo plan for
A couple of weeks at a Tyme. It is crucial to be
Alert and turned "on" and not off in lala land.

Till You Die

Once in your life you'll find true Love
Don't you ever let it slip away,
Do what you have to do to make it last
Don't get caught up in games that people play.

Love doesn't come easy, it takes lots of work
Do what you have to do to find the right one,
Whatever you do give it all that you can
When it's real Love can be so much fun.

To make Love work you must sacrifice
You must work at it every day,
SomeTymes it feels like it's going nowhere
It seems like you're giving it away.

But when life is right and working for you
It feels like it's as easy as pie,
So enjoy every second that Love has to give
Give Love a chance every day till you die.

Today

I tried to get to talk to you today,
But you just kept on talking anyway.
I tried to get a word in edgewise with you,
Still you just keep on talking till my face is blue.
I Love you so much, but you don't let me speak,
Oh, how your bantering leaves me feeling weak.
You have so much to say, but let others have a turn,
I never get to speak, just think what you could learn.
You never listen so I'll write you a letter,
I just hope that it will leave you feeling better.
You say someTymes you wish that you were dead,
I just wish you didn't have those demons in your head.
You say that your life is one big living hell,
You say that someTymes you want to scream and yell.
You just carry on till you start to obsess,
After I listen to you I need to decompress.
I just wish that once that you would take my advice,
You just might find my advice to be quite nice.
What you really need is to have an open mind,
Perhaps your answer is what you might find.
When you start to yelling, you just shut me down,
It just takes my smile and turns it to a frown.
No, I don't like it when we cannot connect,
You just need to listen once to get some self respect.

Toy Balloons

Balloons can move without a sound
Balloons can cheer you up when you're down
Balloons are filled with lots of air
Balloons are fun to give and share.

Balloons come in many sizes and shapes
Balloons are fun to give and take
Balloons are filled with helium gas
Balloons are fun but they don't last.

Balloons are popped with just a pin
Balloons can change the mood you're in
Balloons are given on special days
Balloons can often fly away.

Balloons are fun you just need to blow
Balloons are toys that you can make grow
Balloons are made of Mylar and rubber
Balloons are best when you share them with another.

Tracy

We were always the best of friends
We played together every chance we got
We spent hours just playing as kids do
We liked to spend our free Tyme a lot.

There were Tymes we worked together
There were the days we did your paper route
There were days we spent at one another's home
There were days we just rode our bikes about.

You were the big brother I never had
You made life seem like it had no end
You moved on in your life as we all do
You made me so glad to be your friend.

I wish I could just call you up
I wish we could just talk on the phone
I wish we lived closer together
I wish that I wasn't here alone.

Maybe it's because were now older
Maybe it's because were now apart
Maybe we'll meet up once again
Till then I'll keep you in my heart.

Trees

Trees are a gift from God to man
Trees grow in both dirt and sand
Trees give birds a place to live
Trees are special in the gifts they give

Like logs and wood for us to burn
And paper to write on so we can learn
They grow strong throughout the year
A place that animals hold so dear.

They provide us with the gift of shade
And the things from which trees are made
They give us lumber and wood
The things they give are oh, so good.

A forest is made up of trees
And all their wood and their leaves
They provide us with a place to rest
Of all the plants trees are the best.

Twelve red roses in a vase…they are twelve
Reasons that I Love you. Each one is different
From the others…and like our Love they are
Beautiful and each is distinct. Red and aromatic
They make the room smell so Lovely. Their
Bright red color is a reminder of the way my
Heart is and beats for you…strong and never
To stop its course of action. It continues even
When I am at rest, and it beats in Tyme with
Yours. Their delicate petals are soft and supple
Yet attracts the eye of the beholder and won't
Let go. Just like when you are in my arms I
Never want to let you go. My heart is drawn
To yours and it never lets go of its grasp on
Your soul.…but unlike the flowers which will
Fade away and die over Tyme, my Love only
Grows stronger with the passing of each and
Every day.

My heart beats in Tyme with the ticking of
The clock. Onward and constantly beating
And ticking for now and to forever, and to
Never miss a beat. My heart is a reminder
That like Tyme, it never ends. It strikes the
Hour in a way that give my soul peace as it
Chimes to tell me that yet another yet another
Hour has passed, yet my Love for you beats
On. It hasn't found a need to take a rest. It
Signals to remind my soul it has found another
Reason to express it's wonderful Love for you.
Twenty four Tymes in a day, my heart strikes
A beat that expresses its Love for you. With
Every second that passes is a small reminder
That our wonderful Love for each other moves
Onward and forward to infinity.

It's 2:00 a.m. and all is well except for me.
I'm riding the mania train again and nothing
No nothing will slow me down. My pen will
Not move as fast as my tongue, so I just have
To try to catch up as best as I can. And so it
Goes faster and faster. Just try to catch up if
You can that is. And when you finally get that
Pen in sync with your mouth, you've got to
Write it down as fast as you can. When you
Are on the wild and wicked mania train all
You can do is pray that it will end soon…
But it doesn't. it just speeds away into the
Night…away…away…away. And you, just
What can you do? You just hold on with all
Of your might and try to use caution whenever
You can!

Tyme

Tyme is a way to tell your age
And each day is a separate page
It's a way for measuring your day
Tyme is helpful in so many ways.

Tyme is measured in days and weeks
Tyme is a way in which nature speaks
Tyme is measured in months and years
Tyme is nothing you need to fear.

Tyme is a way to take note of the minutes
Tyme is a clock and you are in it
Tyme goes by so quick and fast
Tyme is a chronology that lasts and lasts,

Tyme rolls by and leaves it's mark
A day is measured from dawn till dark
Tyme leaves its mark upon your face
Tyme's wrinkles are it's only trace.

Until Eternity

You make me feel safe and Loved. Two things
That are hard to find these days. I hope you
Can say the same about me. I Love you so
Very much. So much more than I thought I
Could ever Love somebody. You are my
Heart and soul conceived in Love. Love is
Such a rare and precious thing. I guard my
Heart someTymes because I feel vulnerable.
You make me realize that the world needs
More great people just like you are. I want
To hold you in my heart and make you feel
Loved and adored, because you are. I will
Love you from now till the end of Tyme.
It is a promise that I make to you. I know
That I'll be there from now till eternity comes
And goes. And that's a long, long Tyme.

Up and Down

When I'm feeling sad and down and out,
I get so upset it makes me want to shout.
I get to feeling down and I get to feeling blue,
I am so upset I just don't know what to do.
It's like I'm cold and I just can't get warm,
And all I really want is to be in your arms.
But I'm feeling low, all I can do is cry,
When I'm feeling low all I want is to be another guy.
I'd do anything to stop me from being low,
I want to be happy and for my moods to flow.
Now I can't see the light at the end of the road,
And all I feel like is an old run over toad.
I just want the pain to stop, I want it to go away,
But for that to happen I'll have to wait for another day.
When I'm feeling down all the colors turn to black,
And in myself, it's the happiness that I lack.
When I'm feeling low all I really feel is tired,
But someday soon I'll be feeling way too wired.
When I'm feeling low it's to God that I pray,
That I will be feeling better soon some other day.
And someTymes when I'm low I don't want to eat,
I feel so stiff and sore, it's like I have been beat.
All I really want to do is to stay in bed and sleep,
When the night falls all I do is watch the minutes creep.
And when the day comes that I'm feeling high and manic,
I'll want life to slow down, then I start to panic.
No, it's not fair that I live life so up and so down,
But that's the way life goes, so I just wear a frown.
No, there's no cure for feeling high or feeling blue,
So I'll just have to find some other way to muddle through.

You're gone and you can't hurt me anymore
You're gone…I guess this evens the score,
The other day I heard you'd died
A part of me was glad inside,
I recall the way things used to be
I recall the way you tortured me,
You were so mean, you truly were a witch
You were so mean, your gaze could make me itch,
The way you looked at me, you thought I was a pest
The way you looked at me, could cause my duress,
Of the things you did, you were a control freak
Of the things you did, you loved to hear yourself speak,
You took my confidence and left me without any
You took my pride and screwed the lives of many,
You laughed at my spirit like it was a joke
You crushed my soul with just one stroke,
At night you haunt me, you haunt me in my dreams
At night you haunt me, it makes me to scream,
Now you're gone, you can't hurt me anymore
Now you're gone I guess this evens the score,
It's Tyme for me to let you go
I'm finally done with feeling so low.

Darkness falls in the peak of night
It's all dark and I can't see the light,
While snow is falling to the ground
It lays there cold without a sound.
At night I walk the cold dark streets
I hear the sound of crunching feet,
One must walk through knee deep snow
For there is no other way to go.
It's like a cold nightmarish scene
As I leave the tracks where I have been,
There is no sound to be heard at all
As snowflakes start to begin to fall.
So I leave tracks where I have tread
I'll soon be home and go to bed,
Where I will dream of Summer's lies
As I make my way home as snowflakes fly.
When I'm finally home I warm my feet
While I make something good to eat,
For I am tired of Winter's woes
That's just the way this season goes.

Water

Water is a gift from God above
Water is pure, water is Love
Water is needed for you to live
Water is a gift for you to give.

Water is needed both night and day
Water is needed to grow and play
Water is needed to keep us glowing
Water is needed to keep us growing.

Water is always good to drink cold
Water is important to both young and old
Water is needed by both plant and man
Water is something to keep life grand.

Water is needed by all earth's creatures
Water is needed as an important life feature
Water is important for you to drink
Water is needed to thrive and think.

I wish you were here beside me
I wish you were here to guide me
There's so much that I want to say
Nothing will ever get in my way.

Now you're here and I hold you tight
Holding you makes me feel alright
I just Love to hold your hand
Holding your hand makes me feel grand.

Come over here and sit by my side
Come over here and let me be your guide
There's so many things that we can do
I'll just leave it up to you.

Now it's Tyme to go to bed
Still there's things I haven't said
Pull me close and say good night
Holding you just feels so right.

And in the morning when we wake
There's Tyme for us for Love to make
I'll always want to hold you close
You're the one I Love the most.

He stands there cold, his branches bare
With nowhere to move in the frigid air.
He dreams away the Winter's blues
From the top down to his frozen roots.
He remembers the joy of the Summer's day
As he carried the nest of birds at play.
He thinks of when he was covered in leaves so green
When he was where all of the squirrels had been.
He was home to a group of birds so small
They grew up there as he stood tall.
He misses the joys of Spring Tymes weather
As he was home to a nest of twigs and feathers.
He misses the days of Summer's sun
As he shook his leaves to have some fun.
His roots are deep within the snow
He's now the home to a murder of crow.
For he has no where to move in the Winter's air
He cannot move his cross to bare.

It's Spring again and the fresh air and sun are
Here. It feels like the first day of wonderful
Weather in ages. It feels so great to smell the
Fresh air. The sun seems to be saying "Hello!
Welcome to the best season of the year. It's
Here. Enjoy it because it won't last forever!"
And while I'm enjoying the day the cat is sitting
In the window and letting the gentle breeze blow
Over him. It's so nice to open up all of the
Windows and get some fresh air in the house
Since last Fall. There are just a few clouds in
The bright sunny sky. The sun feels warm on
My face and it's just warm enough to give you
A little color if you take it all in. it's the first
Tyme I've felt the sun in a long, long Tyme.
All of the snow has melted away and there are
Just a few puddles where the snow was not too
Long ago. I've got to enjoy it because we're
Supposed to get some more snow in a couple
Of days from now. But no worries, it won't
Stick around because it's supposed to stay in
The fifties in the next couple of days afterwards.
Hooray for Spring! May the warmth and sunshine
Last forever!

Going to a yard sale can be a lot of fun. You
Never know just what you'll find. I like to
Know just what it is that I am looking for. If
I don't have an idea of what I am looking for
I tend to buy things that I really don't need.
One of the best things about going to yard
Sales or flea markets is that you can some-
Tymes get a better price if you are willing
To dicker or haggle over the price of an item.
I also enjoy hosting a yard sale from Tyme
To Tyme. When you have a yard sale you
Can get rid of things that you no longer have
Use for without throwing them away for
Nothing. I also like to haggle over the price
Of items in my sales. The other great thing
About yard sales is that you can let others
Know about certain things that you are looking
For a specific item and they can help you
Find it. My greatest things that I have gotten
In yard sales are vintage albums to add to
My collection. I Love just searching at an
Auction as well. The best records of my
Collection came from Aunt Diane and my
Mother-in-law Betty. They have found
Some great records over the years.

You are the reason I live for.
You are the one that I Love.
You are so special to me.
You are so handsome and good looking.
You are so strong at heart.
You are the one I Love to talk with.
You are the one I breathe for.
You are the one that I need in my life.
You are the one that makes me happy.
You are the one that makes me strong.
You are the one I share my feelings with.
You are the one that makes me proud.
You are the one that is so caring.
You are the one that is so giving.
You are the one that is so Loving.
You are the one that is so sharing.
You are the one that makes life worth living.
You are the one that is so smart.
You are the one that I share my life with.
You are the one that I share my dreams with.
You are the one that I spend all my Tyme with.
You are the one that is so kind.
You are the one that is all mine.

Even though I am Bipolar and depressed
I have learned that crying doesn't solve
The problem. It is okay to be depressed
But I don't cry about it because it doesn't
Make the situation any better. I feel sad
And depressed and I like to let my feelings
Flow, but of the many moods I have you'll
Never see me cry. I can say that if I need
To let things out I'll do so, but I try not to
Let my feelings show. There are Tymes
When you can get overwhelmed by emotion
And it can make you very upset, but I try
To hold all my emotions inside. I used to
Think that a good cry could cleanse the
Emotions, but I have learned that it is just
Embarrassing to cry in front of others. I
Try to keep all of my emotions to myself
But this can lead to putting all of your
Emotions on the back burner and letting
Them stew for a while. The thing that is
Bad about this is that you never take things
As they happen. You need to let the emotions
Out and deal with them. I have learned that
The best thing is to deal with things as they
Happen. Another thing to do is to let your
Emotions flow on paper. This way you
Deal with them as they occur and that is
Why I have written these books that I have
Written over the years.

Printed in the United States
By Bookmasters